CLASSIC WARPLANES

GRUMMAN
F-14
TOMCAT

Lindsay Peacock

GALLERY BOOKS
An Imprint of W. H. Smith Publishers Inc.
112 Madison Avenue
New York City 10016

A SALAMANDER BOOK

© Salamander Books Ltd. 1990
129/137 York Way,
London N7 9LG,
United Kingdom.

ISBN 0–8317–1400X

This edition published in 1990 by Gallery
Books, an imprint of W. H. Smith Publishers,
Inc., 112 Madison Avenue, New York, New
York 10016.

Gallery Books are available for bulk purchase
for sales promotions and premium use. For
details, write or telephone the Manager of
Special Sales, W. H. Smith Publishers, Inc.,
112 Madison Avenue, New York, New York
10016. (212) 532-6600

CREDITS

Editor: Bob Munro
Designers: Oxprint Ltd, England
Color artwork: TIGA, Michael Keep
(© Salamander Books Ltd)
Three-view and cutaway drawings: © Pilot
Press Ltd, England
Filmset: Flairplan Typesetting Ltd, England;
Oxprint Ltd, England
Color separation: Graham Curtis Repro,
England
Printed in Belgium by Proost International
Book Production

AUTHOR

LINDSAY PEACOCK'S working life has been entirely associated with aviation in one form or another, beginning in 1964 with British European Airways and continuing until after the merger with the British Overseas Airways Corporation which saw the formation of British Airways.

Leaving the latter company in the summer of 1976, he opted to pursue a career as a freelance aviation writer and photographer specializing in military subjects. Since then, he has completed several hundred articles which have appeared in aviation magazines published in the United Kingdom and abroad. He is also the author of a number of books, including the Salamander titles "Strike Aces" and "Aerial Firepower", and has contributed text and pictures to many others.

CONTENTS

THE evolutionary process which culminated in Grumman's F–14 Tomcat taking its place aboard US Navy aircraft carriers from 1974 onwards may be traced back to summer 1961, when US Secretary of Defense, Robert S. McNamara, decided that the US Air Force's requirement for a new strike fighter and the US Navy's search for a new interceptor could be satisfied by a single Tactical Fighter Experimental (TFX) design.

Overruling Navy protestations that service needs would not be satisfied by pursuing this radical concept, the Secretary of Defense pressed ahead with what eventually became known as "McNamara's folly" and chose to purchase separate versions of the General

Dynamics F–111 for each service. Ultimately, the naval derivative proved to be little more than an unmitigated disaster, for, like the Air Force's F–111A, the Navy F–111B suffered from engine- and inlet-related difficulties. Even worse was the fact that it was far too heavy, tipping the scales at a massive 70,000lb (31,750kg) gross weight.

Since the Navy originally specified a gross weight not exceeding 50,000lb (22,700kg), it follows that the F–111B was far from ideal and a succession of weight reduction efforts were implemented. These met with some success but brought their own penalties by compromising cost-saving and commonality aspects that were prime factors in prompting a single design in the first place.

Against this background, Grumman – the sub-contractor responsible for manufacturing part of the F–111B and for final assembly and flight testing – began to explore the possibility

of a replacement embodying many F–111B features. By autumn 1967, work on this project had progressed sufficiently to merit drawing it to the Navy's attention. Although far from being a definitive proposal, the Navy's

The Model 303-60

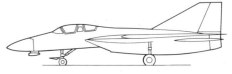

Above: Grumman's Model 303–60 sported a variable-geometry wing and a single large fin. Weapons were to be carried on underwing and underfuselage stations.

The Model 303C

Above: Modification of the Model 303–60 led to several new designs, including the sleek, twin-finned Model 303C. Again, the variable-geometry wing was retained.

The Model 303D

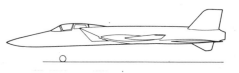

Above: The low-wing Model 303D was a more radical, but unsuccessful, concept. High fuel consumption at cruising speed, poor longitudinal stability and excessive drag led to its demise in April 1968.

Below: I11-suited for the Navy's fighter requirements, the General Dynamics F–111B was cancelled in 1968. In its place, Grumman began work on the F–14 Tomcat.

reaction was favourable, encouraging Grumman to continue refining its preliminary design studies and report on them to the Navy hierarchy.

A subsequent comparative analysis conducted by the service in spring 1968 revealed that Grumman's Model 303-60 was markedly superior to the F-111B, but there were still a few more hurdles to be negotiated before the Grumman proposal was able to

The Model 303E

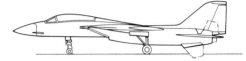

Above: Refinement of early designs led to the Model 303E in June 1968. It featured folding ventral fins, and was to carry four AIM-7 Sparrow medium-range missiles.

The Model 303F

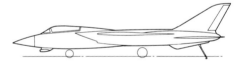

Above: The Model 303F had a large fixed wing, but it wasn't enough. Further analysis was to show that, when armed with six AIM-54s, the 303F was a poor fighter.

The Model 303G

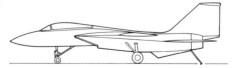

Above: The Model 303G could not carry the AIM-54, and was both lighter and smaller as a result. The US Navy, however, wanted any new fighter to carry six AIM-54s, thus eliminating the 303G.

make the transition from being a promising design to the hardware stage. The first of these was cleared in May 1968 when Congress "pulled the plug" on F-111B funding, essentially killing that project although cancellation did not occur until December 1968.

Even before formal termination of the F-111B, Navy planners, eager to make up for several "lost" years, were drawing up a requirement for a new experimental fleet fighter known as VFX, and this was circulated in July 1968. Having done much groundwork, Grumman was quick to respond to the formal request for proposals. Ling Temco Vought, North American Rockwell and McDonnell Douglas also came up with submissions, as did General Dynamics, clearly not too embarrassed by its experiences with the ill-fated F-111B.

NAVY REQUIREMENTS

In basic terms, VFX called for a tandem, two-seat, twin-engined fighter able to undertake fleet air defence, interdiction and ground attack tasks. In addition, it was to incorporate certain items of equipment from the F-111B programme, most notably the Hughes AWG-9 weapon control system and the AIM-54 Phoenix long-range air-to-air missile (AAM). Other weapons options included AIM-7 Sparrow and AIM-9 Sidewinder AAMs, and an internally-mounted Vulcan M61A-1 cannon.

Operationally, it was to be capable of performing combat air patrol (CAP) tasks at distances of up to 200 miles (322 kilometres) from the parent aircraft carrier for up to two hours at a time. Terms of reference for escort and air superiority missions envisaged a radius of action some 80 per cent greater than that of the McDonnell Douglas F-4J Phantom II, while for interdiction and close air support

Above: Grumman's response to the US Navy's VFX Request for Proposals ran to no less than 37 volumes, occupying 54 binders. All the hard work paid, and Grumman won in January 1969.

(roles which have since been abandoned) it would be able to carry up to 14,500lb (6,576kg) of ordnance. Finally, performance figures stipulated a top speed of around Mach 2.2.

General Dynamics, Ling Temco Vought and North American Rockwell soon fell by the wayside, leaving McDonnell Douglas and Grumman to fight it out. It is probably fair to say that the latter company had the inside track from the outset, although company officials almost certainly had to endure some anxious moments before Grumman was announced as victorious on 15 January 1969.

By no means the least expensive contender, Grumman's candidate was, however, adjudged to offer the best value for money, although political considerations evidently played some part in the decision to go with the New York-based company. Regardless of the reasons which prompted selection of what became the Tomcat, in early February 1969, less than three weeks after being notified of victory, Grumman was awarded a contract covering design, construction and flight testing of an initial batch of 12 F-14As, funding being split between fiscal years 1969 and 1970.

History and Development

Above: Development of the Model 303E eventually led to the F–14, and the mock-up's single-fin soon gave way to the twin-fin arrangement.

Construction of these pre-production machines was still a long way off as the design had by no means been finalized at this stage, even though Grumman had cut metal on some components for the prototype as early as December 1968, confidently anticipating eventual victory. Through spring and summer 1969, further refinement of the Grumman Model 303E took place, with perhaps the most significant change (and certainly the most visible) concerning the decision to abandon the original single fin and rudder assembly which, in conjunction with a folding ventral strake, was to provide directional stability. Navy objections to this arrangement (in particular the folding strake) resulted in the now familiar twin-fin layout with two smaller fixed ventral strakes. This change came too late to appear on the full-size mock-up, although it was soon modified to the definitive twin-tail configuration.

Below: A scale model of the F–14 is readied for another in the long series of low-speed wind tunnel tests of the definitive Tomcat design.

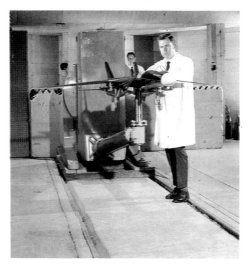

As already noted, Grumman had begun fabrication work as early as December 1968, but the process of manufacture accelerated following the awarding of the initial contract, and the maiden flight was targeted to take place on or before 31 January 1971.

Like many other Grumman products, construction of the prototype took place at the company's Bethpage factory in New York state, and by late summer 1970 Bu.No. 157980 was beginning to take on recognizable form prior to being transported the short distance to Calverton, Long Island.

SECRET JOURNEY

The latter location was to be the centre for initial flight testing, and movement to Plant 7 began in the early morning hours of 25 October 1970, the bulky shape of the first F–14A being shrouded by tarpaulins for the relatively short road journey. On arrival, little time was wasted in setting about final assembly before the complete airframe was subjected to the multitude of ground tests and checks that were necessary prior to it venturing skywards.

On 14 December, with the festive season approaching, the prototype was moved out to the runway for the first time to conduct a sequence of taxi trials. Exactly one week later, those in charge felt that the moment was right to attempt the maiden flight, even though the weather was by no means ideal. For this momentous event, Grumman's chief test pilot, Robert Smythe, was in command, with project test pilot, William "Bob" Miller, occupying the rear cockpit.

Shortly after 1600 hours, they took off successfully but this first flight was brief, Smythe confining himself to just two circuits of the airfield before landing. Completed more than a month ahead of the target date, this timely sortie was perhaps the best Christmas present many of those at Grumman could have hoped for.

Seasonal celebrations were still to be completed when triumph turned to near-tragedy during the Tomcat's second trip aloft, on 30 December. Departing Calverton in mid-morning,

Above: With canopy masking still in place, the prototype F–14A Tomcat emerges fresh from the paint shop at Grumman's Calverton plant.

Smythe and Miller were again in control, but this time their roles were reversed. For the first 25 minutes, all went well, with an initial series of stability and control checks being completed and the undercarriage retracted successfully. Then the pilot of a chase plane reported "smoke" emanating from the Tomcat.

Within moments, it became apparent that the "smoke" was actually hydraulic fluid, Miller reporting failure of the prime hydraulic system. In the normal course of events, this should not have been too serious a problem, but Miller sensibly chose to return to Calverton. For a time, it looked as though their luck was in, an emergency nitrogen bottle being employed to lower the undercarriage at four miles (6.4km) from the airfield; but fate evidently held all the aces that day and the secondary hydraulic system failed seconds later. With control now limited to the Combat Survival Systems (an

emergency measure by which rudders and tailerons may be utilized), Miller continued to nurse the crippled F–14 towards the safety of home base.

He nearly made it, but with barely a mile (1.6km) to go it became apparent to Miller that he was losing the battle to retain control and that the chances of a safe landing were nil. There was no alternative but to eject. Smythe went

Below: On only its second test flight, the prototype F–14A Tomcat crashed as a result of fatigue failure. Both crew members managed to eject and parachute to safety.

first, while the aircraft was just 25ft (7.62m) above the treetops. Miller's departure was even more dramatic -- following Smythe's ejection, the aircraft pitched over into a dive and he parted company with the Tomcat less than half-a-second before it struck the ground.

Despite the fact that both pilots landed near the wreckage, they escaped more or less unscathed, with injuries being confined to a skinned fingertip and a cricked back. Both soon resumed flight test duty, although Miller was to die in another F–14 accident 18 months later. For the observers of the crash, which included the families of both pilots, the last desperate moments of the first Tomcat must have been an horrific ordeal, but less than 30 minutes elapsed before they were reunited.

ACCIDENT INVESTIGATION

For Grumman, as manufacturer, the loss of the prototype must have been particularly worrying, but the ensuing investigation revealed that fatigue failure was the root cause, pipework in both hydraulic systems being affected. Resonance was at the heart of the problem, for it was discovered that, at flight idle, the revolutions per minute (RPM) of both the engine and the hydraulic pump were pitched on the exact frequency that would cause the pipework to vibrate. Within seconds, that vibration would reach such an intensity that failure was inevitable, allowing the precious hydraulic fluid to escape and causing a swift and irretrievable loss of control.

In subsequent tests, Grumman replicated the failure during a ground run by reducing power to the flight idle setting and simply watching the pipe. The engineers didn't have long to wait – it took just nine seconds for fatigue-induced failure to occur. Incorporating a "fix" was a fairly simple matter.

History and Development

Loss of the prototype resulted in some delay, and it was not until 24 May 1971 that flight testing resumed with the second Tomcat (Bu. No. 157981). Once again, Robert Smythe was in command, but this time the outcome was more satisfactory and by the end of the year seven more F-14s had flown from Calverton. With more and more aircraft available, development test flying accelerated throughout 1971.

However, development was not without setbacks, two more prototypes being lost before the Tomcat attained operational status in September 1974. In the first accident, on 30 June 1972, William Miller died when he flew into the waters of Chesapeake Bay while rehearsing his display routine for a charity air show at Naval Air Station Patuxent River, Maryland.

Almost exactly a year later, on 20 June 1973, another prototype was destroyed in quite bizarre circumstances while flying from the Pacific Missile Test Center's base at NAS Point Mugu,

Above: The second Tomcat was fitted with a pair of canard surfaces prior to the start of spin tests in 1972. Also visible in this view is the gun muzzle blast trough.

PRE-PRODUCTION FLEET		
Production Blocks	Quantity	BuAer/Test Fleet Numbers
F–14A–01–GR	1	157980/"1"
F–14A–05–GR	1	157981/"2"
F–14A–10–GR	1	157982/"3"
F–14A–15–GR	1	157983/"4"
F–14A–20–GR	1	157984/"5"
F–14A–25–GR	1	157985/"6"
F–14A–30–GR	1	*157986/"7"
F–14A–35–GR	1	157987/"8"
F–14A–40–GR	1	157988/"9"
F–14A–45–GR	1	157989/"10"
F–14A–50–GR	1	157990/"11"
F–14A–55–GR	1	**157991/"1X"

*Modified to become the sole F–14B

**Was to have been "12", but became "1X" to replace "1" in the test programme following the crash of the first prototype on 30/12/70.

Left: a slow fly-by with everything out reveals the wing leading-edge slats and trailing-edge flaps in the extended position. The wings are shown at 20deg minimum sweep.

Within the next two years, problems with the temperamental Pratt & Whitney TF30 turbofan were directly responsible for the destruction of six more F–14As, and it is only recently that the Navy has been able to obtain a re-engined Tomcat even though the original F–14A was only ever intended to be an "interim" version, paving the way for the F–14B.

POWERPLANT PROBLEMS

While the latter would have embodied an identical avionics suite, it was to have the so-called "definitive" engine, specifically Pratt & Whitney's F401 turbofan. Unfortunately, development difficulties culminated in this potentially much more suitable powerplant being abandoned in spring 1974, much to the chagrin of the US Navy. Rather than have no Tomcat at all, the Navy settled for the lesser evil, namely

Above: In a rare break from the busy test programme, three pre-production Tomcats demonstrate the aircraft's minimum, intermediate and maximum wing sweep settings.

California. Employed on weapons separation trials, it could literally be described as having shot itself down, falling victim to an inert AIM-7E-2 Sparrow AAM which pitched up moments after launch and struck the parent aircraft a mortal blow when it ruptured a fuel tank.

Below: The third pre-production Tomcat was the systems evaluation aircraft, being used to test the communication, navigation and weapons systems.

In neither instance could failure be attributed directly to the aircraft, but two further casualties in 1974 provided uncomfortable pointers to the future. Both were engine-related, the first incident resulting in the second prototype being declared a write-off after a ground fire at Calverton on 13 May. Then, on 19 September 1974, just two days after the USS *Enterprise* left San Francisco for the maiden Tomcat deployment, another engine fire ended the career of the eighth prototype at NAS Patuxent River.

Below: The fourth Tomcat was the first to be fitted with the Hughes AWG–9 FCS and AIM–54 Phoenix AAMs. Note the Phoenix-carrying pallets in the underfuselage "tunnel".

History and Development

Above: Only one F-14B has been produced, this being assigned to a series of engine test programmes. It is seen here taking off under the power of the F401-PW-400.

the TF30, but this marriage of airframe and engine certainly did not turn out to be a happy one.

In 1972, of course, such embarrassments lay in the future, and those closely associated with the F-14 probably had good reason to congratulate themselves on the progress being made as testing was moving ahead rapidly at three major centres of aerial activity. The parent company was responsible for exploring and expanding the envelope from Calverton, making extensive use of an automated telemetry system by which data could be captured, analyzed by computer and presented to engineers and other observers on the ground via cathode ray tubes in real time (i.e. instantaneously).

Use of this facility was instrumental in limiting the duration of the development programme, and progress was undoubtedly aided by the decision to assign a trio of KA-6D Intruders to the project. Modified with a hose-and-drogue assembly to serve as in-flight refuelling tanker aircraft, each was able to transfer up to 20,000lb (9,080kg) of fuel to an airborne Tomcat, thus extending the amount of time that development aircraft could stay aloft and greatly increasing the data "take" from each sortie.

Indeed, in-flight refuelling became so routine that many flights were limited solely by pilot fatigue, and it was not uncommon for up to six fuel transfers to take place during a single mission. Between them, the automated telemetry system and in-flight refuelling support were estimated to have cut 18 months off the development effort; no mean achievement when one recalls just how sophisticated the F-14 Tomcat really is.

TESTING CONTINUES

Other agencies associated with the test programme were located on the east and west coasts of the USA. At NAS Patuxent River, the Naval Air Test Center (NATC) bore the brunt of service evaluations, concentrating mainly on handling qualities and performance. Examination of the AWG-9 fire control systems' functions and capabilities was largely the responsibility of the Naval Missile Center (later redesignated the Pacific Missile Test Center) at NAS Point Mugu, this organisation also conducting an extensive series of trials with live and inert weapons. Each agency operated its own fleet of dedicated test aircraft. Another valuable

Below: Three KA-6D Intruder tankers were to play an important support role in the F-14A test programme, their centreline "buddy" packs being used to transfer fuel to the Tomcats.

Above: Moments after dropping clear of the Tomcat, the AIM–54 Phoenix's rocket motor ignites and blasts the missile towards its target.

PRE-PRODUCTION TEST FLEET TASKS

157980/"1": First flew on 21/12/70. High-speed testing and exploration of flight performance envelope. Lost on 30/12/70 due to hydraulic failure.

157981/"2": First flew on 24/5/71. Low-speed, high angle of attack, and stall/spin testing. Used later for gun trials. Lost in ground fire on 13/5/74.

157982/"3": First flew on 28/12/71. Structural test vehicle used to prove interceptor and fighter envelopes.

157983/"4": First flew on 7/10/71. Fitted with AWG-9 FCS and AIM-54A AAM for systems compatibility evaluations.

157984/"5": First flew on 26/11/71. Systems instrumentation and compatibility testing including navigation, communications, weapons systems, ECM and data link suites.

157985/"6": First flew on 10/12/71. Missile separation and weapon system compatibility testing. Lost on 20/6/73 after being struck by an inert AIM-7E-2 Sparrow AAM.

157986/"7": First flew on 12/9/73. F-14B prototype used to test the F401-PW-400 Advanced Technology Engine. Later used to test the F101DFE (first flew on 14/7/81), for which it was known as the "Super Tomcat".

157987/"8": First flew on 31/12/71. Provided contractual guarantee aerodynamic performance data for full production F-14 configuration. Lost in ground fire on 19/9/74.

157988/"9": First flew on 28/12/71. AWG-9 FCS evaluation work.

157989/"10": First flew on 29/2/72. Carrier suitability proving programme. First catapult launch on 15/6/72. Lost when it struck water in Chesapeake Bay, Maryland, on 30/6/72 while rehearsing for an airshow.

157990/"11": First flew on 6/3/72. Avionics systems testing.

157991/"1X": First flew on 31/8/71. Replaced "1" in high-speed testing and exploration of flight performance envelope.

contribution was made by Air Test and Evaluation Squadron Four (VX–4). Also resident at Point Mugu, this Operational Test and Evaluation Force (OTAEF) unit obtained its first F-14A in late 1972 and has operated the type ever since. Apart from pure test and evaluation taskings, VX–4 was also responsible for preparation of Tactical Manuals to be used by Tomcat communities at NAS Miramar, California, and NAS Oceana, Virginia.

Formal obstacles to be surmounted along the path to service entry were many and varied, but key elements were the three Navy assessments which have to be completed by every type of aircraft and helicopter destined for service use. The first was US Navy Preliminary Evaluation One (NPE 1), which took place less than a year after

History and Development

Begun at NAS Point Mugu on 6 July 1972, NPE 2 (West) was mainly concerned with the Tomcat's AWG-9 weapons control system and associated avionics, and was completed successfully on 23 July. Running more or less concurrently, NPE 2 (East) was largely accomplished from Calverton, with NATC personnel making use of Grumman's Automated Test System in an evaluation which began on 10 July and terminated on 15 August. Handling qualities constituted a key feature, and the ATS was flown with several armament configurations.

FLEET DEBUT

Later that same year, the F-14 began to reach the Fleet, with training squadron VF-124 at NAS Miramar being the first "customer" to take delivery on 8 October. On 14 October, commissioning of the first deployable Tomcat

the maiden flight. Principally concerned with verifying the flight envelope, NPE 1 was less complex than later evaluations and was completed over a two-week period beginning on 2 December 1971.

Another major milestone was passed the following summer when the F-14 earned its sea legs aboard the USS *Forrestal*, with the first catapult launch being accomplished on 15 June 1972. The first arrested landing, or "trap", followed on the 28th of the same month, while the next significant hurdle in the process of being cleared for operational service was NPE 2.

By this time, development flying was really beginning to pick up and NPE 2 was a two-pronged effort, with separate East and West portions. A more ambitious assessment of the Tomcat, it employed the services of four aircraft and several hundred personnel from the NMC and the NATC, as well as key contractors such as the Hughes Corporation and Grumman.

Above: In mid-1972, sea trials were conducted aboard the USS *Forrestal*. Hooked up to the steam catapult, this Tomcat starts to hurtle down the deck and into the air.

Below: A graphic illustration of the problem facing a Navy pilot when it comes to landing aboard a carrier at sea. Use of the airbrake helps cut the approach speed.

squadrons (VF–1 and VF–2) took place at the same base; an exciting event, but one which did not disguise the fact that the F–14 still had some way to go before it could be declared fully operational.

That declaration came one stage nearer in autumn 1973 when the F–14 cleared the obstacle posed by Board of Inspection and Survey (BIS) trials. The most demanding assessment yet, BIS thoroughly examined all aspects of the aircraft, with test objectives embracing everything from deck-handling qualities through perform-ance characteristics to operation of the complex AWG–9 fire control system and associated weaponry. Such a multi-discipline evaluation naturally called upon the expertise of various specialists, and NMC and NATC per-sonnel clearly bore the brunt of the workload.

Below: Just where a pilot doesn't want a Tomcat – on his tail. The widely-spaced engine intakes are seen to advantage in this view, as is the narrow cross-section of the fuselage nacelle.

In truth, it would have been highly surprising had they not done so, since they had been intimately involved in assisting the Tomcat to make the tran-sition from being a promising new-comer to a fully-fledged weapon of war. That achievement was eventually realized in the surprisingly short span of less than four years and both Grum-man and the Navy had good reason to

Above: Though it is a big beast, the wing oversweep facility helps reduce the amount of hangar space taken up by the Tomcat.

celebrate in September 1974 when the Tomcat began its maiden deployment aboard the Navy's premier aircraft car-rier, namely the nuclear-powered USS *Enterprise* (CVN-65).

COLLOQUIALLY known as the "Iron Works", Grumman has built up an enviable reputation for producing carrier-borne aircraft, and the Tomcat is just the latest in a long line of immensely durable warplanes, being a fitting successor to such classic naval fighters as the F6F Hellcat and F9F Cougar.

Like many modern warplanes, however, what eventually emerges from the assembly facility at Calverton on Long Island is the sum total of work undertaken not only by Grumman itself, but also by a multitude of sub-contractors and equipment suppliers spread across the length and breadth of the United States. Indeed, when it comes to the basic airframe structure, some sub-assemblies are actually fabricated by companies which could, until a few years ago, have safely been described as competitors. Thus, while the finished article may rejoice in the Grumman name, it should not be forgotten that a host of other concerns may reasonably claim credit for supplying the Navy with what is probably the most potent fighter it has ever had.

TOMCAT ASSEMBLY

Responsibility for assembly is entrusted to Grumman's Plant 6 at Calverton, and it is here that the many and varied components which go into making a Tomcat come together and take on recognizable form before emerging into the open as a complete structure. The job of manufacture begins long before that stage is reached though, with key sub-assemblies being prepared elsewhere before being brought together at Plant 6.

Before examining the assembly process, it is worth looking at some aspects

of the manufacturing process, beginning with Grumman's contribution. This is centred upon Bethpage (Plants 1, 2 and 3), and it is here that most of the structure takes shape, before delivery to Calverton. The biggest single sub-assemblies are the forward and mid-fuselage sections which are eventually mated at Plant 6, but other component parts which find their way to the Calverton plant include the aft fuselage assembly.

Responsibility for manufacture of the aft fuselage is entrusted to Fairchild-Republic at Farmingdale, Long Island, while another member of that group provides the fin and rudder assemblies which are produced at Hagerstown, Maryland. Engine inlet

Right: Two spherical bearings are used to pivot the variable-sweep wings. Should one bearing fail, the other is strong enough to hold the wing unit together.

Above: The Tomcat begins to take shape as the major fuselage sub-assemblies are mated at Grumman's Calverton facility.

ducting and aft nacelles are supplied by Rohr Industries, with other companies which make a substantial contribution including B. F. Goodrich (wheels, tyres and brakes), Martin-Baker (ejection seats), Bendix (landing gear), Brunswick (nose radome),

Swedlow (canopy/windshield), Garrett AiResearch (environmental control system, temperature control system, cabin pressure system and engine starter) and Hughes (AWG–9 fire control system).

As far as possible, sub-assemblies are transferred to Calverton complete with electronic and other key sub-systems already in place so as to simplify the task of actually putting each Tomcat together. In broad terms, final assembly is a seven-stage process, starting at Station A where mating of the nacelle assembly to the forward/mid-fuselage module occurs, as well as the mating of inlet/glove and aft fuselage/nacelle assemblies and fitment of the cockpit canopy. At Station 1, the main landing gear is fitted so as to permit the Tomcat to move through the remaining stages of assembly on its own wheels. Fin and rudder assemblies are also added at this stage, as are the fuel cells, final hydraulic components and cockpit instrument displays.

At Station 2, the engines (either TF30s or F110s) are installed and wing

Below: To facilitate its progress through the rest of the assembly plant, the landing gear is added to the aircraft at Station 1. All three units retract forward.

and horizontal tail surfaces are added, resulting in the aircraft being fundamentally complete, with only overwing fairings, ejector seats, nose radome and weapons system "slave" units (missile rails and the like) to be added. In addition, the first of an impressive array of functional checks are conducted. These include preliminary testing of the hydraulic system and an air leak check of the fuel system.

From here on, Plant 6 activities are mainly concerned with verifying that everything operates as it should, work at Station 3 involving rigging, a hydraulic functional test and boresight alignment, while Station 4 examines the performance of critical avionics items including the AWG–9 fire control system. After that, the now largely complete F–14 moves outside to Station 5 for engine runs, fuel calibration and taxi tests before going to the paint shop at Station 6. Once that stage is complete, newly finished Tomcats

Above: By the time the F–14 leaves Station 2 at the Calverton plant, the major assembly work on the aircraft has been completed.

come the responsibility of Plant 7, where weapons pylons and rails are added and the integral Vulcan gun is tested, it being necessary for all aircraft to fire 500 rounds before final delivery.

Flight acceptance testing follows, still under the auspices of Plant 7, with an average of three flights being necessary prior to Navy acceptance by means of Defense Department Form 250. After that, it is usual for the military acceptance team at Calverton to log one or two further sorties before turning the aircraft over to the ferry crews who will fly them to operational stations for squadron assignment.

Turning to the structure itself, construction is essentially conventional with little in the way of composites,

Tomcat Structure

save for boron-epoxy which is used as a skin material on the horizontal tail surfaces, or "tailerons". Probably the most significant single structural member is the single-cell titanium box beam, a 22–foot (6.71m) long component which transmits wing loadings to the fuselage via two sets of wing pivots, and which also serves as an integral fuel tank. Built up from some 33 machined items, the box is unique in

Left: At Plant 7, 500 rounds are fired from the integrally-mounted M61A1 to test its abilities and alignment. The 20mm six-barrel cannon can fire its load of 675 shells at a rate of 6,000 rounds per minute.

Grumman F-14A Tomcat cutaway drawing key

1 Pitot tube
2 Radar target horn
3 Glass-fibre radome
4 IFF aerial array
5 Hughes AWG-9 flat-plate radar scanner
6 Scanner tracking mechanism
7 Ventral ALQ-126 deception jamming antenna
8 Gun muzzle blast trough
9 Radar electronics equipment bay
10 AN/ASN-92 inertial navigation unit
11 Radome hinge
12 In-flight refuelling probe (extended)
13 ADF aerial
14 Windscreen rain removal air duct
15 Temperature probe
16 Cockpit front pressure bulkhead
17 Angle of attack transmitter
18 Formation lighting strip
19 Cannon barrels
20 Nosewheel doors
21 Gun gas vents
22 Rudder pedals
23 Cockpit pressurization valve
24 Navigation radar display
25 Control column
26 Instrument panel shroud
27 Kaiser head-up display (HUD) unit
28 Windscreen panels
29 Cockpit canopy cover
30 Face blind seat firing handle
31 Ejection seat headrest
32 Pilot's Martin-Baker GRU-7A ejection seat
33 Starboard side console
34 Engine throttle levers
35 Port side console panel
36 Pitot static head
37 Canopy emergency release handle
38 Fold-out step
39 M61A1 Vulcan 20mm six-barrel rotary cannon

40 Nose undercarriage leg strut
41 Catapult strop link
42 Catapult strop, launch position
43 Twin nosewheels
44 Folding boarding ladder
45 Hughes AIM-54A Phoenix air-to-air missile (six)
46 Fuselage missile pallet
47 Cannon ammunition drum (675 rounds)
48 Rear boarding step
49 Ammunition feed chute
50 Armament control panels
51 Kick-in step
52 Tactical information display hand controller
53 Naval Flight Officer's instrument console
54 NFO's ejection seat
55 Starboard intake lip
56 Ejection seat launch rails
57 Cockpit aft decking
58 Electrical system controller
59 Rear radio and electronics equipment bay
60 Boundary layer bleed air duct
61 Port engine intake lip
62 Electrical system relay controls
63 Glove vane pivot
64 Port air intake
65 Glove vane housing
66 Navigation light
67 Variable area intake ramp doors
68 Cooling system boundary layer duct ram air intake
69 Intake ramp door hydraulic jacks
70 Air system piping
71 Air data computer
72 Heat exchanger
73 Heat exchanger exhaust duct
74 Forward fuselage fuel tanks
75 Canopy hinge point
76 Electrical and control system ducting
77 Control rod runs

78 UHF/TACAN aerial
79 Glove vane hydraulic jack
80 Starboard glove vane, extended
81 Honeycomb panel construction
82 Navigation light
83 Main undercarriage wheel bay
84 Starboard intake duct spill door
85 Wing slat/flap flexible drive shaft
86 Dorsal spine fairing
87 Fuselage top longeron
88 Central flap/slat drive
89 Emergency hydraulic generator
90 Bypass door hydraulic jack
91 Intake bypass door
92 Port intake ducting
93 Wing glove sealing horn
94 Flap/slat telescopic drive shaft
95 Port wing pivot bearing
96 Wing pivot carry-through (electron beam welded titanium box construction)
97 Wing pivot box integral fuel tank
98 Fuselage longeron/pivot box attachment joint
99 UHF data link/IFF aerial
100 Honeycomb skin panelling
101 Wing glove stiffeners/dorsal fences
102 Starboard wing pivot bearing
103 Slat/flap drive shaft gearbox
104 Starboard wing integral fuel tank (total internal capacity 2,364 US gal/8,949 litres)
105 Leading edge slat drive shaft
106 Slat guide rails
107 Starboard leading edge slat segments (open)
108 Starboard navigation light
109 Low-voltage formation lighting
110 Wing tip fairing

111 Outboard manoeuvre flap segments (down position)
112 Port roll control spoilers
113 Spoiler hydraulic jacks
114 Inboard, high lift flap (down position)
115 Inboard flap hydraulic jack
116 Manoeuvre flap drive shaft
117 Variable wing sweep screw jack
118 Starboard main undercarriage pivot fixing
119 Starboard engine compressor face
120 Wing glove sealing plates
121 Pratt & Whitney TF30-P-412 afterburning turbofan
122 Rear fuselage fuel tanks
123 Fuselage longeron joint
124 Control system artificial feel units
125 Tailplane control rods

126 Starboard engine bay
127 Wing glove pneumatic seal
128 Fin root fairing
129 Fin spar attachment joints
130 Starboard fin leading edge
131 Starboard all-moving tailplane
132 Starboard wing (fully swept position)
133 AN/ALR-45 tail warning radar antenna

134 Fin aluminium honeycomb skin panel construction
135 Fin-tip aerial fairing
136 Tail navigation light
137 Electronic counter-measures (ECM) antenna
138 Rudder honeycomb construction
139 Rudder hydraulic jack
140 Afterburner ducting
141 Variable area nozzle control jack
142 Airbrake (upper and lower surfaces)
143 Airbrake hydraulic jack

144 Starboard engine exhaust nozzle
145 Anti-collision light
146 Tail formation light
147 ECM aerial
148 Port rudder
149 Beaver tail fairing
150 Fuel jettison pipe
151 ECM antenna
152 Deck arrester hook (stowed position)

153 AN/ALE-29A chaff and flare dispensers
154 Nozzle shroud sealing flaps
155 Port convergent/divergent afterburner exhaust nozzle
156 Tailplane honeycomb construction
157 AN/ALR-45(V) tail warning radar antenna
158 Tailplane boron fibre skin panels

159 Port wing (fully swept position)
160 All-moving tailplane construction
161 Tailplane pivot fixing
162 Jet pipe mounting
163 Fin/tailplane attachment mainframe
164 Cooling air louvres
165 Tailplane hydraulic jack
166 Hydraulic system equipment pack

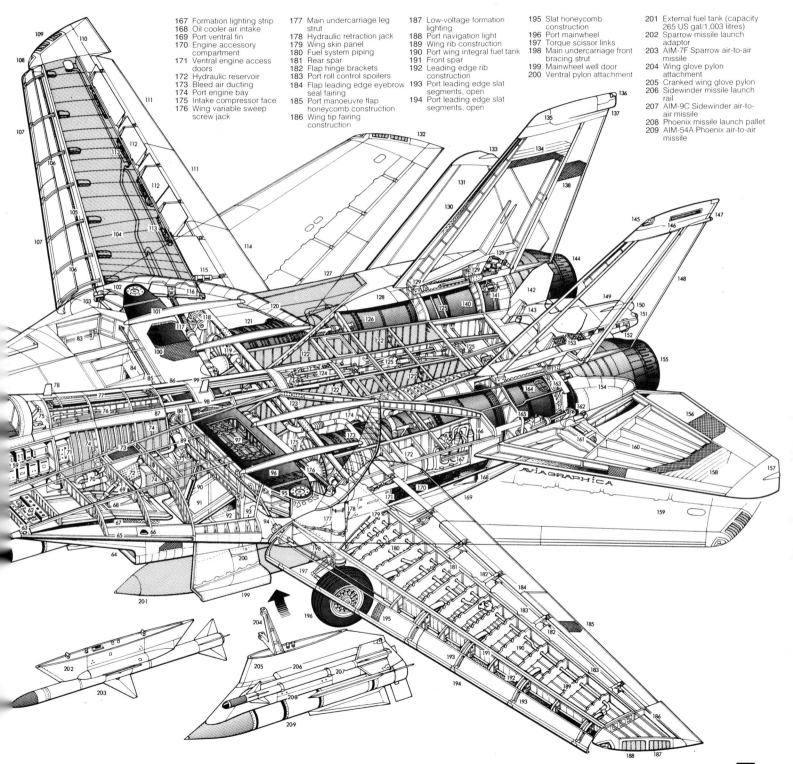

Grumman F–14 Tomcat

167 Formation lighting strip
168 Oil cooler air intake
169 Port ventral fin
170 Engine accessory compartment
171 Ventral engine access doors
172 Hydraulic reservoir
173 Bleed air ducting
174 Port engine bay
175 Intake compressor face
176 Wing variable sweep screw jack

177 Main undercarriage leg strut
178 Hydraulic retraction jack
179 Wing skin panel
180 Fuel system piping
181 Rear spar
182 Flap hinge brackets
183 Port roll control spoilers
184 Flap leading edge eyebrow seal fairing
185 Port manoeuvre flap honeycomb construction
186 Wing tip fairing construction

187 Low-voltage formation lighting
188 Port navigation light
189 Wing rib construction
190 Port wing integral fuel tank
191 Front spar
192 Leading edge rib construction
193 Port leading edge slat segments, open
194 Port leading edge slat segments, open

195 Slat honeycomb construction
196 Port mainwheel
197 Torque scissor links
198 Main undercarriage front bracing strut
199 Mainwheel well door
200 Ventral pylon attachment

201 External fuel tank (capacity 265 US gal/1,003 litres)
202 Sparrow missile launch adaptor
203 AIM-7F Sparrow air-to-air missile
204 Wing glove pylon attachment
205 Cranked wing glove pylon
206 Sidewinder missile launch rail
207 AIM-9C Sidewinder air-to-air missile
208 Phoenix missile launch pallet
209 AIM-54A Phoenix air-to-air missile

19

Tomcat Structure

that it marked the first use of the electron beam welding technique on a modern warplane. Four pin joints are all that is necessary for attachment to the fuselage, while the wing pivots consist of two annular, spherical bearings made largely of titanium alloy with Teflon-type surfaces.

Fuselage sections are built up around machined frames, with steel being employed for the aft section and undercarriage support frame plus the spectacle beam on which rear engine and "taileron" mountings are located.

Fuel tank locations

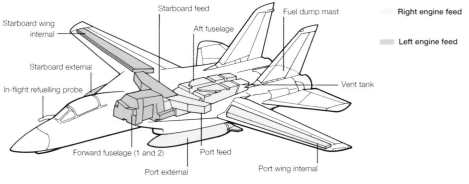

SPECIFICATION

F–14A Tomcat

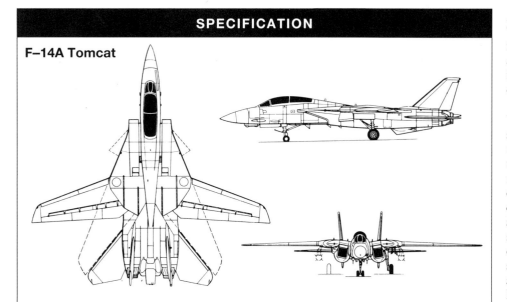

Dimensions
Length: 62ft 8in (19.10m)
Height: 16ft 0in (4.88m)
Wing span: (unswept) 64ft 1½in (19.54m)
        (swept) 38ft 2½in (11.65m)
        (overswept) 33ft 3½in (10.15m)
Tailplane span: 32ft 8½in (9.97m)
Gross wing area: 565sq ft (52.49m²)

Weights
Empty: 40,104lb (18,191kg)
Normal take-off weight: 58,571lb (26,567kg)
Maximum take-off weight: 74,349lb (33,724kg)
Maximum external weapons load: 14,500lb (6,577kg)

Power
2 × Pratt & Whitney TF30–P–414A afterburning turbofans

Maximum thrust: 29,000lb (93kN)
Internal fuel: 16,200lb (7,348kg)
External fuel: 3,800lb (1,724kg)

Performance
Maximum level speed, high-level: Mach 2.34 (1,544mph 2,458km/h)
Maximum level speed, low-level: Mach 1.2 (912mph 1,468km/h)
Carrier approach speed: 154mph (248km/h)
Minimum take-off distance: 1,400ft (427m)
Maximum rate of climb, at sea level: +30,000ft/min (9,140m/min)
Service ceiling: +50,000ft (15,240m)
Maximum range, with external fuel: 2,000 miles (3,220km)
Minimum landing distance: 2,900ft (884m)

Above: Six internal tanks allow the Tomcat to carry 16,200lb (7,348kg) of fuel. In addition, external drop tanks add another 3,800lb (1,724kg); and in-flight refuelling is possible via the extended probe.

With regard to the external fuselage skin, bonded honeycomb panels are most commonly used, though not in the region of the engines. Here, titanium is the standard material by virtue of the fact that it is better suited to coping with heat. The same material also serves for upper and lower wing skins and offers the added advantage of being highly corrosion-resistant, something that is always welcome on aircraft which routinely operate in salt-laden atmospheres.

SKIN MATERIAL

Further applications of bonded honeycomb material may be found in the inlet duct sidewalls, leading and trailing edges of the wing, movable control surfaces and the glove vanes, while the vertical tail surfaces embody honeycomb sandwich skins. Returning to titanium, this can also be found in the engine intakes, hydraulic lines, main and rear fuselage longerons and the engine support beam. Finally, as already noted, boron-epoxy serves as a skin material on the "tailerons".

Turning to the question of propulsion, most Tomcats still rely on the Pratt & Whitney TF30 afterburning turbofan, a powerplant which has suffered from more than its fair share of problems. Improvement initiatives

Below: Four major variants of Pratt & Whitney's TF30 turbofan engine have been used by the Tomcat over the years. This is a TF30–P–414, which superceded the –412/–412A in quantity production.

have meant that no fewer than four variants have been fitted to the F–14A throughout its service career. The maximum power output of 20,900lb (9,489kg) in afterburner has remained constant through the TF30–P–412, –412A, –414 and –414A variants, with most of the changes that have been incorporated being intended to increase reliability and durability, as well as to limit damage in the event of turbine blades being "thrown" as a result of failure.

Above: The sturdy main landing gear has to take a lot of hard punishment every time the F–14 makes a "trap". Liberal use of steel provides much-needed strength.

At long last, however, the Navy has managed to satisfy its desire to obtain a re-engined Tomcat, and recent deliveries have been of the F–14A(Plus) version which is fitted with a pair of General Electric F110–GE–400 afterburning turbofans, each of which has a

TF30-P-414 turbofan engine

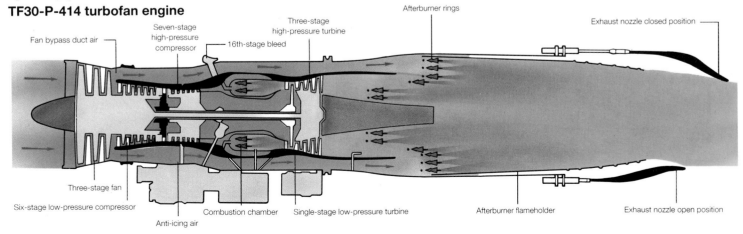

Tomcat Structure

Above: An unusual view of one of the Tomcat's engine bays, seen looking forward from the extreme rear of the aircraft.

offer additional area during the take-off and landing flight regimes. Operation of these ramps is programmed as a function of Mach number to automatically provide the correct airflow throughout the entire flight envelope, with boundary layer air being diverted via a throat-bleed slot through doors on the upper wing surface. Exhaust nozzles on the F–14A are of the convergent/divergent (con/di) type, which is evidently doubly beneficial by virtue of possessing a lower installed weight and offering superior performance at speeds of between Mach 1.5 and Mach 2.0.

Turning to the variable-geometry wing, sweep angle is controlled automatically by the Mach sweep programmer and is a function of Mach and

Below: The Tomcat's massive, box-like engine intakes are acutely raked back, and set slightly away from the sides of the fuselage. Splitter plates are not fitted.

maximum dry rating of 23,100lb (10,487kg). In addition to 38 new-build examples, 32 existing F–14As are to be upgraded to this standard, and the same engine is also to be fitted to the F–14D in conjunction with a much-revised avionics suite.

AIR INTAKES

Air is passed to the widely separated engines via two-dimensional air intakes, the outboard location of which prevents sluggish boundary layer air from being ingested and thus eliminating the need for splitter plates. Once in the inlet "tunnel", air is compressed by forward-facing, variable-position ramps which over-collapse in order to

Above: A graphic illustration of the Tomcat's widely-spaced, convergent/divergent engine exhaust nozzles: the port nozzle is closed for normal military power, and the starboard nozzle is fully dilated for afterburning power settings.

Below: In addition to slats and flaps on the wing, the Tomcat has a pair of triangular surfaces known as glove vanes. These are deployed to improve supersonic stability when the aircraft is operating at speeds of Mach + 1.4.

Glove vane mechanism (starboard wing)

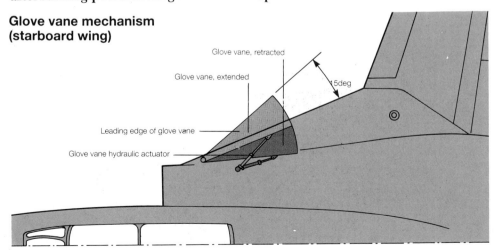

Glove vane, retracted

Glove vane, extended

15deg

Leading edge of glove vane

Glove vane hydraulic actuator

altitude. In flight, sweep angles measured at the leading-edge vary from 20deg to 68deg, and it is also possible to employ an "oversweep" setting of 75deg when on the ground. Designed as a space-saving measure, the latter reduces span to 33ft 3.5in (10.15m) and is of great value at sea where deck-space is always at a premium.

Also worthy of mention are the glove vanes, these being small canard surfaces which swing out from the leading edge of the fixed centre section of the wing. Both manual and automatic modes of operation exist, the latter coming into play at speeds in excess of Mach 1.4, while an inhibiting device restricts extension to five degrees with the wings in the fully-spread position. Maximum extension is 15deg (relative to the wing leading-edge) and is achieved at sweep angles exceeding 35deg. Suitable for use in either subsonic or supersonic flight, they are

Tomcat Structure

mainly intended to enhance lift during in-flight manoeuvring, but they also alleviate loads on the "tailerons" at high speed. It should, however, be noted that this feature has been deleted from both the F–14A(Plus) and the F–14D.

Moving on to more conventional moving surfaces, the F–14 possesses single-slotted trailing-edge flaps which are split into three sections on each outer wing panel. Inhibiting devices prevent operation at certain sweep angles, with the two outer main segments becoming inoperative once 50deg of sweep is attained, while the inner auxiliary section cannot function at sweep angles in excess of 22deg. In addition to their primary lift-generating function at low speed, the outer sections can also double as

Left: New equipment and displays cannot disguise the fact that the pilot's cockpit is rather dated.

Below: Pitch control is enhanced on take-off by the deflection of the all-moving "tailerons".

with two ventral fins to provide directional stability, while control in pitch and roll is furnished by the fully-variable "tailerons" which operate in unison for pitch and differentially for roll.

Hydraulic power comes courtesy of two main systems, but there is also a back-up system. This is designed to provide sufficient control in pitch and yaw to enable a crew to recover safely in the event of both primary systems being rendered unusable. Electrical power is provided by two 60/75 KVA generators, each being capable of producing enough current to operate all of the F–14's systems. As a back-up, a hydraulically-driven 5 KVA generator will develop sufficient emergency power to get a crew and their stricken aircraft home safely.

Left: The RIO's "office" features a large digital display unit as part of the AWG–9 FCS.

Below: To cut approach speed to a minimum, this Tomcat has its upper speedbrake fully opened.

manoeuvring flaps. Lift-augmenting devices are completed by wing leading-edge slats.

Other moving surfaces comprise spoilers and air brakes, with the former consisting of independent pairs situated on the upper surface of each outer wing panel. Inadvertent operation is prevented by mechanical locking devices once the wing-sweep angle exceeds 62deg. Air brakes are found on the upper and lower fuselage boat tail surfaces between the jet nozzles, and once again, an inhibiting device limits maximum deflection of the lower unit so as to ensure sufficient ground clearance when the undercarriage is in the deployed position.

Finally, there are the vertical and horizontal tail surfaces. Twin fin and rudder assemblies work in conjunction

DESPITE the fact that much of the radar and weapons package of the F-14A is fundamentally of sixties-vintage and was conceived for the F-111B, it is still capable of spoiling anyone's day. Certainly, the Tomcat is the only fighter in the world with the potential to engage and destroy targets at ranges which greatly exceed 50 miles (80.5km).

At the heart of this impressive capability is the Hughes Aircraft Company which was responsible for designing and manufacturing both of the ele-

Below: The wide-angle perspective accentuates the excellent degree of visibility afforded to the crew of a Tomcat. Rear-view mirrors on the canopy frame help the pilot to visually "check his six".

ments that permit the Tomcat to engage opponents at such extreme distances, namely the AN/AWG-9 weapons control system and the AIM-54 Phoenix air-to-air missile. More recently, a revised radar package has been conceived and developed for the F-14D, but the AWG-9 suite is still the primary system and merits close attention.

Changes necessary to permit AWG-9 integration into the F-14 centred around the switch from a side-by-side to a tandem crew arrangement and the need to use shorter-range weaponry like the AIM-7 Sparrow, AIM-9 Sidewinder and Vulcan M61 20mm cannon; but it was also specified that information relating to firing envelopes for these weapons be presented on the pilot's head-up display (HUD) unit.

The need to undertake some redesign to accommodate the change from the F-111B to the F-14A was perhaps a negative aspect, but the lengthy gestation brought with it some compensatory factors as a result of improvements in technology, particularly in the area of miniaturization. These are best illustrated by savings made in weight and volume, the former falling from about 1,760lb (800kg) to 1,235lb (561kg), while the latter dropped from $0.87m^3$ to $0.78m^3$.

Since the Tomcat's primary function is that of destroying enemy aircraft, it follows that the AWG-9's main tasks relate to detecting, tracking and ranging, but it may also provide data for use in air-to-ground modes even though these are not routinely utilized. Elements of the package include the

radar antenna, cockpit displays, a secure two-way data link, a television sighting unit and computers to process the wealth of data prior to it being presented to the crew.

The radar scanner itself is a 36in (91.4cm) planar-array type with an effective range of around 150 miles (241km). It is capable of operation in three modes, specifically search, track and attack, and presents information on the evolving tactical situation to the back-seat Radar Intercept Officer (RIO) by means of a 12in (30.5cm) diameter video display unit (VDU).

At extreme ranges and for attacks with the Phoenix missile, the radar operates in a pulsed-Doppler mode, while for medium and short-range encounters a conventional pulse mode is used, the latter being employed to provide target illumination for the AIM–7 Sparrow AAM which is only able to home successfully on targets that are being "painted" continuously. Deployment of the "fire-and-forget" AIM–120A Advanced Medium-Range Air-to-Air Missile (AMRAAM) will eliminate this requirement and in turn render the F–14 itself less vulnerable.

In normal operation, as many as 24 targets can be tracked simultaneously although a single Tomcat would not, of course, be able to deal with all of these. When target ranges diminish to about 115 miles (185km), the associated computers are able to provide information relating to closure rates and assign threat priority. RIOs are advised of this by cues presented on the VDU, other data offered including direction of target travel and Identification Friend or Foe (IFF) "squawks", which in theory allows them to recognize friendly aircraft.

Right: The awesome capabilities of the AWG–9 FCS and AIM–54 Phoenix AAM are obvious in this illustration of one F–14's attack on six high-speed target drones.

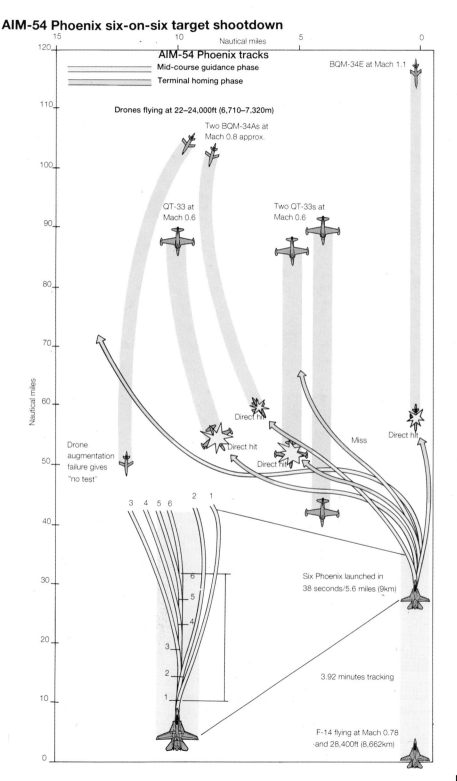

AIM-54 Phoenix six-on-six target shootdown

Tomcat's Eyes and Claws

Three modes of operation are provided for close combat situations – vertical scan lock-on, boresight and manual lock-on. The latter two are self-explanatory, while for the first, the radar antenna functions only in pitch, scanning a narrow swathe and locking on automatically to any target within a five mile (8km) radius. Information relating to weapons launch parameters in all three close combat modes is conveyed to the pilot via the HUD unit and is continually updated by computer.

Finally, there is the Track-While-Scan (TWS) facility which is used for multiple target tracking and multi-Phoenix engagement situations. In TWS, as many as 24 targets may be tracked, with threat priorities being established by computer. The system also assigns specific weapons to specific targets and advises crew members when the best missile launch position has been reached.

AWG-9 FCS modes

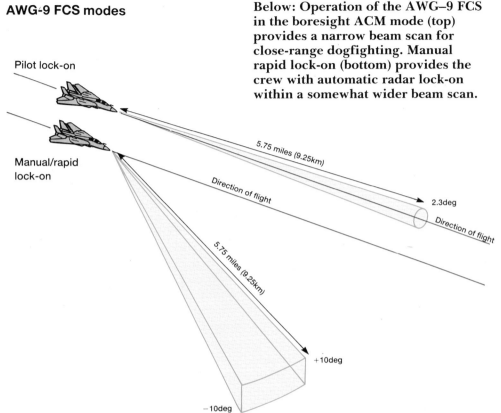

Pilot lock-on

Manual/rapid lock-on

5.75 miles (9.25km)

Direction of flight

2.3deg

Direction of flight

5.75 miles (9.25km)

+10deg

−10deg

Below: Operation of the AWG–9 FCS in the boresight ACM mode (top) provides a narrow beam scan for close-range dogfighting. Manual rapid lock-on (bottom) provides the crew with automatic radar lock-on within a somewhat wider beam scan.

Above: Located under the Tomcat's nose, the RIO-operated Northrop TCS can provide positive target identification at distances well beyond visual range.

More prosaic AWG–9 capabilities include navigation, gun direction, air-to-ground calculations and a built-in test (BITE) facility which permits it to monitor its own performance and that of associated equipment. Faults are automatically brought to the attention of the crew.

Although able to detect targets by radar, there are situations in which a visual identification is necessary if US rules of engagement are to be met. Unfortunately, the "Mark One eyeball" is not perhaps the finest sensor in terms of range, and it is for this reason that most F–14s now carry a Television Camera Sight (TCS). Occupying space originally filled by a less than effective infra-red detection set, Northrop's TCS has proved its worth on numerous occasions, allowing

crews to obtain positive identification at ranges which exceed those of the human eye by a factor of ten.

Moving on to weaponry, compatibility with the Phoenix AAM gives the Tomcat the potential to destroy targets at ranges far in excess of any of its contemporaries, and it is for this reason alone that it must stand head and shoulders above comparable interceptors. In the Navy's eyes, it is desirable to eliminate enemy aircraft long before they can reach a position from which they might pose a threat to the well-being of the Carrier Battle Group. Operating in the Barrier Combat Air Patrol (BarCAP) role, the Phoenix and the Tomcat give the Navy that ability, and in the normal course of events it seems probable that BarCAP elements would be positioned up to 200 miles

(322km) from the parent carrier with in-flight refuelling being used to extend patrol time.

Since the AWG–9 allows the F–14 to engage up to six targets more or less simultaneously, it follows that the maximum load of Phoenix that may be carried is six: four in the "tunnel" between the engines and two more on underwing pylons. In this configuration, the F–14 may also tote two AIM–9 Sidewinders for close-in combat, these being located on "shoulder" rails outboard of each wing pylon.

MAIN ARMAMENT

At over $1 million per round, the Phoenix isn't cheap; but nor are capital ships, so the investment must be seen as worthwhile. Nevertheless, we are talking "megabucks" here, cost projections of a few years back anticipating an outlay of a cool $4.1 billion to buy 3,467 examples of the AIM–54C. In view of that, it is hardly surprising that the Phoenix is not routinely carried. Nor should one be too startled to learn that live firing opportunities are limited to one or two missiles per squadron per annum.

Formal development of Phoenix actually began with the dawn of the "swinging sixties", concept formulation leading to a 1960 competition to find a new long-range weapon. Study of the various contenders resulted in Hughes being awarded a development

Above: A maximum of six AIM–54 Phoenix AAMs can be carried aloft by the Tomcat: two on cranked wing glove pylons, and four on separate semi-conformal pallets located under the fuselage.

and test contract in August 1962, with airborne trials following some three years later. At that time, the Phoenix was intended for the F–111B and early testing was accomplished from one F–111B and two suitably modified Douglas A–3 Skywarriors.

The eventual outcome of these trials provided proof that not everything associated with the F–111B was totally disastrous, for the AIM–54 survived to become the main item of armament for the Tomcat. At the start of the test

Left: To clear the Tomcat safely, the Phoenix is ejected through the surrounding airflow by the use of explosive charges.

effort, unguided missiles were expended, and it was not until 1966 that fully-guided prototype XAIM–54s became available, the very first test of one of these offering startling evidence of the new weapon's potential when it succeeded in hitting its target at a range double that of the best missiles then in service.

Testing was a lengthy process and Hughes did not receive a production contract until December 1970. By then, the Phoenix was earmarked for the Tomcat, so the long interval was probably beneficial in that it allowed "bugs" to be ironed out prior to the weapon attaining squadron service in late-1974.

Production of the AIM–54A version spanned some ten years and roughly 2,500 had been completed by 1981. By that time, a second model – the AIM–54B – had also been deployed, manufacture of this beginning in 1977. Improvements were intended to bestow

Tomcat's Eyes and Claws

Weapon loads

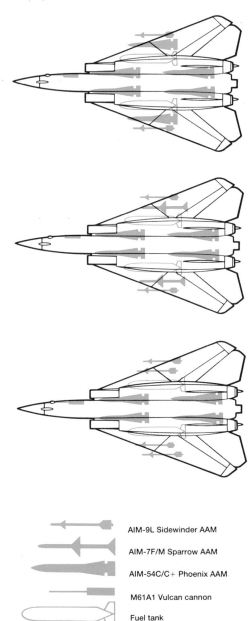

AIM-9L Sidewinder AAM

AIM-7F/M Sparrow AAM

AIM-54C/C+ Phoenix AAM

M61A1 Vulcan cannon

Fuel tank

Above: Each of the weapon loads illustrated provides the Tomcat with no less than eight possible missile "kills", as well as the close-range back-up provided by the M61A1 six-barrel cannon.

enhanced reliability, with perhaps the most noteworthy change concerning guidance equipment which was now all-digital. Environmental conditioning and hydraulic systems were also modified, while the original honeycomb wings and fins of the AIM–54A gave way to components fabricated from sheet-metal.

Improving reliability still further was also the prime factor in development of the AIM–54C, which was started by Hughes with company funds in autumn 1976. "Captive" testing began shortly before the end of the decade, with the first launch following in June 1980. Embodying greater resistance to electronic countermeasures (ECM), the AIM–54C is also superior in terms of accuracy and range; but efforts at improving this impressive weapon haven't been allowed to stop there.

Optimized for deployment on the F–14D, the AIM–54C+ replaced the AIM–54C as the production version in March 1986 and differs primarily by virtue of featuring a self-contained, closed-cycle cooling system, unlike earlier models which were dependent upon a flow of coolant from the parent aircraft. Earlier versions may still be employed by the F–14D, but the lack of a cooling system necessitates some restriction in performance to limit the effects of aerodynamic heating.

SPARROW STATUS

When it comes to encounters at medium-range, the Tomcat is certainly no slouch either although capability has perhaps been compromised by dependence on the AIM–7 Sparrow AAM, a missile that seems to be lacking in reliability. Evidence to support this contention is provided by the most recent US–Libya fracas in which three Sparrows were fired, only one of which appears to have "guided" successfully. Introduction of the new

AIM–120A AMRAAM is expected to eradicate shortcomings in this area, although this "fire-and-forget" weapon has not exactly enjoyed a trouble-free development. Damning evidence of shortcomings is provided by a 1988 General Accounting Office report which stated that "the combat performance of the missiles to be produced for the inventory is uncertain".

For the moment, then, the Sparrow constitutes the Tomcat's principal medium-range weapon, variants in Navy use consisting of the AIM–7E, AIM–7F and AIM–7M. The latter is the current production model and is essentially a marriage of the heavier warhead and larger rocket motor of

Above: A big and heavy missile, the Phoenix is equipped with a fragmentation-type warhead which can be configured for impact– or proximity-detonation. Top speed of the missile is at least Mach 3.8.

the AIM–7F with an advanced mono-pulse seeker head offering better Electronic Counter-Counter Measures (ECCM) capability and enhanced look-down/shootdown potential. Looking to the future, a new model to be known as the AIM–7P is under development, funded by a $19.6 million contract awarded to Raytheon by the US Navy in 1987. Assuming it attains quantity production, it looks like being a vast improvement, with better guidance electronics plus a new fuse device and onboard computer; but plans to buy a "fire-and-forget" version designated AIM–7X appear to have been all but abandoned.

Finally, there is close-in combat, in which either the internal gun or the heat-seeking AIM–9 Sidewinder AAM would be used. As far as the Sidewinder is concerned, this missile's capabilities are very much a known quantity, the AIM–9L having demonstrated its potential for destruction during the first encounter between the US Navy and Libya back in August 1981.

Since then, further refinement has resulted in new models and this long-serving weapon looks like being around for the foreseeable future. At the time of writing, the current production version is the AIM–9M, but shortcomings in acquisition range and ECCM performance will be addressed by the AIM–9R which is slated to enter service in 1992. Initially designated AIM–9M(PIP), development began in 1986 and it will be the first to employ an imaging infra-red (IR) target seeker head.

Should the Tomcat be drawn into a "knife" fight (i.e. combat at very close range) there is always the single General Electric M61A1 Vulcan cannon installed on the port side of the nose, along with 675 rounds of 20mm ammunition. So far, no one has had to use it in aerial combat, but air-to-air gunnery is a routine facet of training and pilots are expected to demonstrate

Above: An excellent view of the Tomcat's undersides, revealing the wing glove and underfuselage weapon stations. Note the pairs of AIM–9L Sidewinder AAMs.

proficiency in live firing exercises against towed banner targets.

One other aspect of weaponry does deserve brief mention, for it is not generally realized that the Tomcat still possesses the potential to perform

interdiction and close air support missions. As it has turned out, the F–14 has never been called upon to undertake either role, but the original requirement stipulated it should carry up to 14,500lb (6,583kg) of conventional ordnance, as well as a pair of AIM–9 Sidewinders for self-defence. As a result, development test flying did examine its capabilities in the air-to-ground arena, and there is no doubt that the Tomcat could be employed for such tasks if the tactical situation warranted it and permitted it. However, since Tomcat aircrew do not appear to train in the disciplines required for air-to-ground operations, it would probably take some time to bring them "up to speed" so this capability must be viewed as a latent one.

In contrast, the Tomcat's potential for reconnaissance is very real, with

Left: Though first and foremost a Fleet defence fighter, the F–14 was designed with a ground attack capability, as evidenced by this shot of a Tomcat equipped with seven Snakeye bombs.

Tomcat's Eyes and Claws

just over 50 F–14As having been configured to carry the Tactical Air Reconnaissance Pod System (TARPS), and it is usual for one squadron on each aircraft carrier to number three reconnaissance-dedicated aircraft amongst its 12-strong complement when at sea. Containing a forward-facing KS–87B frame camera and a side-facing KA–99 panoramic camera, as well as an AN/AAD–5A imaging infra-red sensor and associated environmental control equipment, TARPS entered development in April 1976 and made its ocean-going debut with VF–84 in 1981.

Less than a year later, following the demise of the last front-line Vought RF–8G Crusaders, TARPS became the primary tactical reconnaissance system and has proved its value on numerous occasions, most notably in the Lebanon and during the US invasion of Grenada. Indeed, it is now such a valuable asset that TARPS-compatibility is to be built into all F–14Ds.

Below: TARPS is equipped with a frame camera for vertical and oblique coverage, a panoramic camera, and an IR line-scanner.

Above: When deployed, the TARPS pod is carried on the Tomcat's starboard rear underfuselage station. Normally, three F–14s within the 24 assigned to a Carrier Air Wing (CVW) are configured to carry the reconnaissance pod.

Readers may recall that the F–14A was initially perceived as an interim solution to the Navy's need for a new fleet fighter, the original plan anticipating delivery of just over 60 copies of this TF30-powered machine. Production was then to switch to the "definitive" F–14B which would have been fitted with a pair of Pratt & Whitney F401 turbofans. Ground testing of the F401 began in September 1972, with flight trials getting under way a year later on 12 September 1973, when the seventh Tomcat (Bu. No. 157986) took to the skies for the first time.

Fitted with one TF30 and one F401, the flight test programme soon revealed problems and the Navy eventually chose to abandon work on the new engine. With the F401 a non-starter, the Navy had little option but to stick with what it already had. Progressive improvement of the engine did much to eradicate its worst vices, and TF30 variants were installed in no less

Tactical Airborne Reconnaissance Pod System (TARPS)

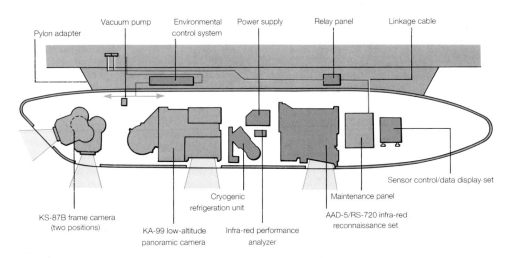

Pylon adapter

Vacuum pump

Environmental control system

Power supply

Relay panel

Linkage cable

Sensor control/data display set

Maintenance panel

AAD-5/RS-720 infra-red reconnaissance set

Infra-red performance analyzer

Cryogenic refrigeration unit

KA-99 low-altitude panoramic camera

KS-87B frame camera (two positions)

than 557 aircraft before F–14A production ended. No mean achievement for an "interim" engine.

Today, the US Navy at last has the new engine that it hoped for at the outset, in the shape of General Electric's F110. Ironically, though, plans to procure a substantial number of new-build aircraft with this powerplant are unlikely to reach fruition, the Tomcat being one type targeted to bear the brunt of cuts in US defence spending. As a result, it seems that fewer than 60 production examples will be completed with the F110.

The bulk of these will bear the designation of F–14A(Plus), being virtually identical to the baseline F–14A. Apart from the new engine, they lack glove vanes but do feature an array of radar warning receiver (RWR) antennae on the underside of the wing adjacent to the glove area.

Thereafter, new-build Tomcats will be completed to F–14D standard with revised avionics and radar as well as the F110 engine, these improvements being intended to permit the Grumman fighter to remain a fully effective element of US seaborne air power until well into the 21st Century. Unfortunately for Grumman, it appears that very few F–14Ds will roll from Calverton before production ends in December 1991.

The overall picture isn't perhaps quite as bad as it may at first appear, for the Navy will be implementing a conversion in lieu of procurement programme (CILOP) in which the existing F–14As will be updated to F–14D configuration. By the time this is completed in about 1998, the Navy will possess an all F–14D fleet and should be in pretty good shape as it enters the next century.

Towards the end of the 1970s, the vexed question of poor engine reliability again raised the desirability of switching to a new powerplant, but once again money proved to be the main obstacle and it was not until early in the next decade that any real progress was made. At the heart of this initiative was the General Electric F101–X (later redesignated F101DFE, signifying "derivative fighter engine"), itself nothing more than a version of the F101 which had been chosen for Rockwell's B–1B strategic bomber.

"SUPER TOMCAT"

To enable flight testing to be accomplished, the F–14B was resurrected from storage during 1981 and fitted with two of the new engines, but it was clear more or less from the outset that this programme was very much a low-key one. Indeed, the number of engines built was limited to just five, comprising two F101–X prototypes and three F101DFEs. Between them, they were to be subjected to ground trials at the General Electric facility at Evendale, Ohio, and the Naval Air Propulsion Test Center at Trenton, New Jersey, before being cleared to venture skywards in the F–14B or, as Grumman chose to call it, the "Super Tomcat".

Flight trials began on 14 July 1981, and continued through the winter of 1981–82 before the F–14B was again placed in store. By that time, it had logged some 50 sorties and 70 hours of flight time in a demonstration programme which confirmed that it was markedly superior to the F–14A with regard to performance. Instances of

Below: With the extra punch from the General Electric F101DFE (seen here in the port engine bay), the F–14B acquired the appropriate title of "Super Tomcat" during the engine trials programme.

Tomcat's Eyes and Claws

Above: Flight-testing of the new F101DFE commenced in July 1981, and it was soon clear that the extra power it offered could significantly improve the Tomcat's overall performance capabilities.

this superiority are provided by CAP loiter time which rose by some 34 per cent, and there was also a 62 percent gain in the aircraft's deck-launched intercept radius.

Encouraged by these and other potential benefits, it was hardly surprising that further development was ordered and General Electric began work on this project in October 1982, the new variant being known as the F110. At that time, the Navy chose to "hedge its bets" since Pratt & Whitney was also working on a rival engine project known as the P1128N. This seemed equally promising, but it would not have been available for service until about 18 months after General Electric's contender. In the end, the US Air Force moved first, ordering a version known as the F110–GE–100 on 3 February 1984. Earmarked for the McDonnell Douglas F–15 Eagle and General·Dynamics F–16 Fighting Falcon, the USAF's decision obviously

influenced the Navy which followed suit less than a week later when it announced that the F110–GE–400 was to power a new Tomcat derivative to be designated F–14D.

Testing of the new engine and airframe pairing began in 1986, with the long-serving F–14B again being heavily involved in its development. A second aircraft (Bu. No. 161867) was added in spring 1987. The latter machine (a converted F–14A) was actually the F–14D prototype but was initially concerned mainly with engine trials so as to permit deployment of the F–14A(Plus). When that phase of the test programme was complete, it would move on to tasks associated with the new suite of avionics and other equipment to be embodied in the F–14D.

After more than a decade of service, and with no new fighter in prospect, the US Navy was understandably anxious to ensure that the Tomcat would remain a viable and effective warplane for the foreseeable future; something that was by no means guaranteed if the existing weapons control system was retained. In consequence, in July 1984, the Navy awarded Grumman a $984 million contract to undertake a major improvement project. Part of that effort entailed adoption of the F110 engine, but a substantial amount of money was set aside for improvements to the radar package as well as other key items of avionic equipment.

What resulted was the Hughes AN/APG–71 radar, fundamentally nothing more than a digital version of the existing radar portion of the AWG–9. Building on lessons learned with the AWG–9 as well as the F–15 Eagle's AN/APG–70 radar, the AN/APG–71 offers a number of gains and benefits. For a start, it has additional operating modes, including monopulse angle tracking, digital scan control, target identification and raid assessment, these features being incorporated in a

Above: Successful trials led to a production version of the F101DFE, known as the F110–GE–400. Tomcats thus equipped sport a new style of engine exhaust nozzle.

package which is in some ways less complex than its predecessor. Certainly, maintenance should be easier, for the number of "boxes" associated with the system has been cut from 30 to 14.

IMPROVED CAPABILITIES

In terms of capability, the features mentioned above should result in a vastly improved Tomcat. For instance, monopulse angle tracking allows targets to be precisely located within the radar beam, something that facilitates operation in the raid assessment mode whereby specific aircraft in a formation may be individually observed. Digital scan control allows better management of the antenna scan pattern, most notably in TWS (track-while-scan) mode since it enables the radar to monitor the overall tactical situation by taking "time out" from normal tracking functions. Finally, the all-important task of target identification will be achieved by analyzing radar returns. This offers

multiple benefits: it will overcome the failings of existing IFF (identification friend or foe) systems which can easily be fooled, and it will do away with the need for an interrogative IFF system, in the process cutting down the number of emissions that an enemy might home in on.

"Hardening" initiatives aimed at bestowing enhanced performance in an intense ECM environment include low-sidelobe antenna and sidelobe-blanking guard channel, frequency agility and a new programmable signal processor. In conjunction with other improvements, these provide better all-round performance.

Grumman's latest Tomcat concept is targeted to meet Navy interceptor needs into the 21st Century and is

fundamentally nothing more than a low-risk alternative to the navalized version of the USAF's Advanced Tactical Fighter (ATF), hence the decision to adopt the designation Tomcat 21. At the moment, this is little more than a proposal, and with production of the F–14D almost certain to be drastically curtailed the probability of Tomcat 21 ever achieving hardware status must be considered low.

According to Grumman, if a go-ahead is forthcoming, the Tomcat 21 could be flying in just three years time, with production specimens joining the fleet three years after that. Since the current time-scale of the USAF's ATF programme anticipates it beginning to enter service in 1995–96 and full operational deployment following in 1996–97, and since development of a Navy derivative would inevitably add four or five years to those dates, Tomcat 21 appears at first glance to be an attractive proposition. Sadly for Grumman, Navy reaction has been lukewarm to say the least, and unless there is a drastic change in attitude the F–14D will almost certainly be the last Tomcat variant to serve with the US Navy.

Below: Though the Navy's future fighter needs are based around a version of the Advanced Tactical Fighter (ATF), Grumman proposed an improved and enhanced version of the F–14, known as the Tomcat 21. Sadly, it has been cancelled.

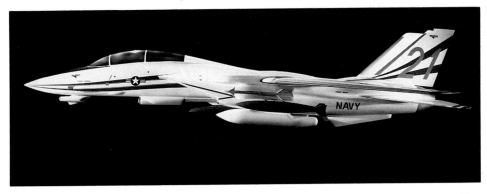

THE process of Fleet introduction began on 8 October 1972 with the delivery of Tomcat Bu. No. 158617 to the master jet base at NAS Miramar. Situated a few miles from San Diego, Miramar is better known to Naval aviators as "Fightertown", and the arrival of the F–14A was a momentous event in that it signalled the beginning of the end for the lines of F–4 Phantom IIs and F–8 Crusaders that occupied apron space at this huge base.

Retirement of these veterans from front-line service was to take some time to achieve, but for personnel assigned to Navy Fighter Squadron VF–124, the hand-over ceremony was a step in the right direction and enabled them to get their hands on an example of the most potent fighter ever to join the US Navy.

Previously equipped with the F–8 Crusader, VF–124 was one of a small number of Navy outfits referred to as Fleet Replacement Squadrons (FRS) although they are generally known as "RAGs", this unflattering term being a hangover from the era of the Replacement Air Group organizations which existed within each major Fleet, namely Atlantic and Pacific. VF–124's selection as the first F–14 training squadron came in 1970, when it was directed to prepare for the new fighter, but it was not until August 1972 that it turned over responsibility for Crusader training to another unit at NAS Miramar.

Essentially, each "community" within the naval aviation framework is concentrated at a single base. Thus, Pacific Fleet fighter squadrons are based at NAS Miramar when not deployed aboard aircraft carriers, while their Atlantic Fleet counterparts use NAS Oceana, Virginia.

Above: The first operational Navy squadron to receive the Tomcat was VF–124 "Gunfighters", one of whose Tomcats is seen here off the coast of California.

In the past, it was not unknown for each major fleet to introduce new warplanes into service more or less simultaneously. Today, however, combat aircraft are so sophisticated that this is no longer really practicable, and it is usual for initial deployment to be assigned to one of the two Fleets. For the Tomcat, that honour fell to the Pacific Fleet and, specifically, to VF–124, which was the only F–14A FRS until late 1975.

SQUADRON SERVICE

Within days, another significant event took place at Miramar when the first two squadrons to employ the F–14 in an operational capacity were commissioned. VF–1 and VF–2 were the units concerned, and they came into being amidst due ceremony at Miramar on 14 October 1972.

For the first few months of their existence, they remained firmly under the parentage of VF–124 for classroom and practical "hands-on" instruction in the Tomcat. By the end of June 1973, however, this phase of training was more or less complete, an event marked by the reassignment of both squadrons to Carrier Air Wing Fourteen (CVW–14) on 1 July 1973.

Simultaneously, both squadrons began independent training operations, each using four Block 65 Tomcats on a kind of "temporary loan" basis from VF–124. By the end of 1973, with the flow of new aircraft from Calverton beginning to pick up, both squadrons had begun to acquire their own Tomcats, and by late April 1974, each was fully equipped with 12 F–14As from Block 70 production.

Thereafter, training activity accelerated as VF–1 and VF–2 worked hard to achieve combat-ready status in anticipation of making the maiden deployment with the Tomcat later that year. This process involved becoming "carrier qualified" and there were a number of short "shake-down" cruises, but proficiency in other areas was also honed throughout summer 1974. Weapons training featured prominently and the opportunity was taken to expend live missiles. VF–1, for instance, conducted a number of "missile shoots", with one F–14A simultaneously launching examples of the AIM–7F Sparrow and AIM–54A Phoenix at a target drone. This "belt and braces" approach certainly had the desired objective, for the drone was destroyed.

By 12 September 1974, all was ready and both squadrons left Miramar, each taking a dozen Tomcats north to the Naval Air Station at Alameda, near San Francisco. There, adjacent to one of the piers at the naval base, lay the huge USS *Enterprise* (CVN–65), the nuclear-powered aircraft carrier that was to be their sea-going home for the next eight months. Other elements of CVW–14 also converged on Alameda, including Grumman A–6 Intruders and EA–6B Prowlers from NAS Whidbey Island, Washington, Grumman E–2 Hawkeyes from NAS North Island, California, and Vought A–7 Corsair IIs from NAS Lemoore, California, and it naturally took some time to lift CVW–14's 80-odd aircraft aboard by crane.

On 17 September, all was ready for departure, the "*Big E*" slipping her moorings at 1000 hours and inching clear of the dockside before heading for the Golden Gate Bridge and the

Right: As a VF–2 "Bounty Hunters" Tomcat awaits its turn, a VF–1 "Wolf Pack" aircraft is hoisted aboard the USS *Enterprise*.

Tomcat in Service

Pacific Ocean. Her destination was the Western Pacific (WestPac), where she was to operate as part of the 7th Fleet.

For the Tomcat, the deployment was perceived to be particularly successful, and it is perhaps not widely realized that this tour of duty provided the F–14 with its first exposure to combat operations. Cruising in the South China Sea during the last desperate days of the Vietnam War, both fighter squadrons furnished combat air patrol (CAP) cover for the evacuation of Saigon in late April 1975. Codenamed "Frequent Wind", this helicopter-borne operation resulted in 5,000 eva-cuees being brought out before Saigon fell, VF–1 and VF–2 making a modest contribution in completing about 20 CAP sorties. As it transpired, the Tomcat did not employ its weaponry on this occasion even though some aircraft came under fire from 37mm anti-aircraft artillery, with minor damage evidently being inflicted on one of the Tomcats.

CARRIER OPERATIONS

Other positive aspects of this first cruise concerned the AWG–9 weapon control system which performed satisfactorily even though mean time between failure (MTBF) levels were less than the 22-hour figure specified. Excellent contractor support minimized the impact, with faulty line-replaceable units simply being removed and replaced. Diagnostic examination of the defective component using on-board versatile avionic shop test (VAST) equipment was often followed by corrective measures, this helping to maintain a good proportion of aircraft at combat ready status.

The aircraft itself also performed well, close to 3,000 hours being accumulated by the two squadrons in some 1,700 sorties. Weaponry was subjected to exhaustive examination, with the AIM–54A Phoenix under very close

Above: Closely watched by deck crew aboard the "Big E", a VF–2 Tomcat makes its final approach. Note the fully-extended arrester hook, ready to snag a deck wire.

scrutiny. Four were fired during the cruise and these generally performed well, three scoring direct hits on targets at ranges from 25 to 53 miles (40 to 85km).

Certainly, these were encouraging signs, and in summing up the cruise, CVW–14's boss, Cdr. John R. Wilson, said, "there is no question that the addition of the F–14 to the *Enterprise*'s air wing made that carrier the world's most powerful warship". Rear Admiral Leonard A. Snead (Commander, Fighter and Airborne Early Warning Wing Pacific) went further when he commented that it "was the most singularly successful fleet introduction of a sophisticated aircraft the Navy ever had".

Much of that praise was justifiable, but it can now be seen to have been perhaps a trifle overblown although in the euphoria of the moment that is probably excusable. In the hysteria surrounding the return of VF–1 and VF–2 to Miramar on 19 May 1975, difficulties with the Pratt & Whitney TF30 engine seem to have been conveniently overlooked, but there can be little doubt that this was responsible

for many a furrowed brow in some very high places.

Intimations that all was not well with the engine had already manifested themselves in the form of a couple of ground fires, but matters worsened when fan blade failures necessitated emergency landings at San Clemente Island and NAS Patuxent River in the latter half of 1974. On those occasions the crews kept their feet dry, but four personnel from VF–1 had to face the indignity of an enforced "ducking" in early 1975.

The new year was only two days old when the first incident occurred, engine failure being responsible for the destruction of a VF–1 F–14A (Bu. No. 158982) soon after take-off from NAS Cubi Point in the Philippines. Eventually, despite the best efforts of the crew, an uncontrollable fire forced them to eject, but they were quickly recovered tō recount their misfortune which apparently began with a "thump", was followed by a "bang", and terminated with a fire.

Less than two weeks later, on 13 January, another VF–1 aircraft (Bu. No. 159001) fell victim to the "thump-bang-fire" syndrome, and once again the crew had no option but to eject. Within hours, the Tomcat fleet was grounded, and it was not until mid-March that flight activity approached levels achieved before the accidents.

In the interval, engineering personnel performed detailed inspections of the TF30–P–412A turbofans; a lengthy process but one which achieved the desired objective, for no more aircraft were lost. Inevitably, though, serviceability rates fell, the magnitude of the problem being best exemplified by the fact that VF–2 completed over 100 engine changes in a matter of weeks.

Had it been feasible to salvage the lost VF–1 aircraft, the cause would probably have been established quickly. Unfortunately, it was not, and the Navy had to wait almost six months before it got the evidence it needed when an F–14A from VF–143 (Bu. No. 159432) suffered an engine fire on take-off from NAS Oceana. Subsequent examination of the hulk (and, in particular, the engines) revealed microscopic manufacturing defects in fan blades supplied to Pratt & Whitney by a sub-contractor.

In time, fatigue failure would occur and the blade would separate, with dire results for the adjacent structure which included fuel lines and tanks. "Fixes" were eventually incorporated in a new version of the engine known as the TF30–P–414 which embodied steel containment casings around the first three fan stages, as well as using a different type of titanium alloy in blade manufacture. Efforts to minimize the fire hazard included provision of more fire extinguishers, titanium sheeting over the engine nacelles

and use of ablative material. TF30–P–414 installation was accomplished fleet-wide between February 1977 and June 1979.

Long before that, VF–124's expertise had been called upon by several more squadrons as they transitioned to the Tomcat. The next customers to report to "school", at the beginning of 1974, were Atlantic Fleet squadrons VF–14 and VF–32. Returning to NAS Oceana in summer 1974, they spent most of the next year in becoming wholly familiar with their new mounts before returning to sea duty in late June 1975.

Operating as part of the Atlantic Fleet's premier Air Wing – CVW–1 – they claimed the distinction of introducing the Tomcat to Mediterranean

Below: A brace of VF–32 "Swordsmen" Tomcats banking gently over the Mediterranean Sea during the unit's initial deployment with the new fighter in 1975.

waters with the 6th Fleet aboard the USS *John F. Kennedy* (CV–67) and by all accounts enjoyed a spectacularly successful tour, notwithstanding a brief grounding due to engine-related problems soon after leaving Norfolk, Virginia. About the only event which marred this deployment was the loss of a VF–14 machine when an arrester wire snapped on recovery. Happily, the crew ejected safely.

For VF–32, this cruise was capped by the award of the prestigious Admiral Joseph Clifton trophy, given annually to the US Navy fighter squadron adjudged to have demonstrated superior performance – something that they probably brought to VF–14's attention in no uncertain fashion!

In truth, of course, the two squadrons aboard the *Kennedy* operated very much as a team and CVW–1's pairing racked up an impressive record in several North Atlantic Treaty Organization (NATO) and non-NATO exercises. Perhaps the high point came in

Tomcat in Service

"Lafayette", when defending fighters were pitted against SEPECAT Jaguar A and Dassault Mirage III strike aircraft of the French Air Force. In 91 attempts to penetrate the fighter screen and "attack" the parent carrier, the French forces were forestalled on every occasion.

Three months after the *Kennedy* got back to Norfolk, two more Atlantic Fleet squadrons headed out to sea, these being VF–142 and VF–143 which sailed aboard the USS *America* (CV–66) in April 1976. The culmination of a transition programme which had begun at NAS Miramar in late summer 1974, this cruise featured the usual round of military exercises as well as some rather more serious business, both squadrons furnishing CAP cover for Operation "Fluid Drive".

Then, as now, events in the Lebanon periodically tended to dominate world headlines, and that was certainly the case in late July 1976 when ships and helicopters of the 6th Fleet carried out "Fluid Drive". In a potentially hazardous operation, they evacuated some 300 US civilians from Beirut, which had been battered by artillery exchanges between various warring factions. Overhead, Tomcats stood ready to pounce on any fighter which attempted to intervene. In the end their services were not needed, and they were to come no closer to combat before returning to NAS Oceana.

COMBAT-READY

For the next four years, combat opportunities were non-existent, and the Navy directed most of its attentions to the continuing re-equipment programme which, by the end of 1979, had seen eight more squadrons convert to the Tomcat. Grumman's warplane now enjoyed primacy when it came to fighter resources, the veteran F–8 Crusader having disappeared from the front-line in 1976, while the F–4 Phantom II was in decline, remaining active with just eight squadrons. Nevertheless, the F–14 had still to experience full-blown combat, and had the April 1980 attempt to rescue the Iranian hostages met with better fortune, it is probable that Tomcats from VF–41 and VF–84 aboard the USS *Nimitz* (CVN–68) would have covered the withdrawal. As history records, the recovery operation ended in tragedy at "Desert One" and the Tomcat had to wait for the chance to use its weapons in anger.

That moment came on 19 August 1981, when two Tomcats from the USS *Nimitz* took less than a minute to reduce the Libyan Air Force's complement of Sukhoi Su–22 Fitter–Js by two. The root cause behind this brief encounter lay in Libya's attempt to claim territorial rights over much of the Gulf of Sidra (sometimes known as the Gulf of Sirte). Since the USA would only accept the more common three-mile (5km) limit, and since the *Nimitz* had been directed to enter the disputed area for a two-day exercise in which live surface-to-air and air-to-air missiles would be expended against drone targets, it follows that the stage was set for confrontation.

Day one of the exercise (18 August) was marked by repeated Libyan attempts to interfere and observe, with Mirages, MiG–23 Floggers, Su–22 Fitters and MiG–25 Foxbats all being encountered by naval aviators. Apart from efforts to gain a tactically advantageous position, the Libyan pilots had not been too aggressive.

On day two, the Libyans were up early as they continued their disruptive efforts, but it looked as though the previous day's pattern would prevail. Certainly, VF–41's boss, Cdr. Henry "Hank" Kleeman, was not expecting much excitement when, accompanied by RIO Lt. David Venlet, he launched from the *Nimitz* soon after 0600 hours in "Fast Eagle 102". In "Fast Eagle

Below: As a VF–84 "Jolly Rogers" Tomcat blasts off the angled deck, a VF–41 "Black Aces" machine is prepared for launch.

Grumman F–14 Tomcat

Below: This VF–142 "Ghost Riders" F–14A displays typically colourful US Navy squadron markings from the late–1970s. The base camouflage was gull grey (upper surfaces) and white (lower surfaces).

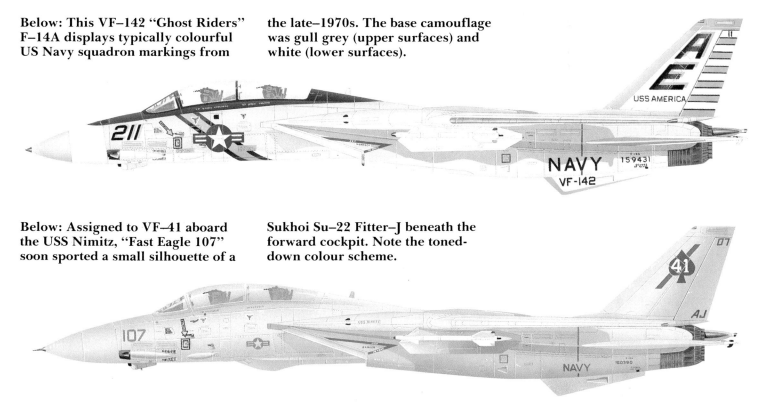

Below: Assigned to VF–41 aboard the USS Nimitz, "Fast Eagle 107" soon sported a small silhouette of a Sukhoi Su–22 Fitter–J beneath the forward cockpit. Note the toned-down colour scheme.

107", Lt. Lawrence "Music" Musczynski and RIO Lt. JG James "Amos" Anderson also left *Nimitz* for an early CAP. On launch, these two Tomcats were destined for different CAP areas, but since Musczynski had no wingman, Kleeman was instructed to rendezvous with "107" and he took responsibility for leading the two-aircraft element as it headed out to a CAP station some 20,000 feet (6,100m) above the sea to the south of the parent carrier.

At 0715 hours, Kleeman and Musczynski were probably beginning to think about returning to the *Nimitz* when Lt. Venlet reported an unidentified radar contact getting airborne

Right: Wearing the green of Islam as its national insignia, this is a Libyan Arab Republic Air Force Sukhoi Su–22 Fitter–J. Though it is a potent fighter, it is no match for the mighty Tomcat.

from the air base at Gurdabya to the south. Within moments, it was clear this contact was heading directly for the Tomcats and also climbing to the same altitude. Alerting *Nimitz*'s combat information centre (CIC) to this "threat", Kleeman and his wingman were instructed to intercept and they duly accelerated and headed south, so as to forestall any attempt at a Libyan break-through.

A "loose deuce" formation was being employed by the two F–14s, with Musczynski flying more or less in line abreast roughly 10,000 feet (3,050m) to starboard of Kleeman, although he soon climbed to position himself about 4,000 feet (1,220m) higher. As the formations closed at a speed in excess of 1,000 knots, the Tomcats made several attempts to introduce an element of "offset", but each attempt was

Tomcat in Service

forestalled by a corresponding change of heading by the opposing fighters (it was now clear that there were two "bogies"), Libyan Ground Controlled Intercept (GCI) direction being particularly good.

At about eight miles (13km) range, visual contact was made by Kleeman, and the "bogies" were identified as Sukhoi Su–22 Fitter–Js. They were maintaining fairly close formation with no more than 500 feet (152.5m) separation. Then, as the two Tomcats began a left-hand turn to manoeuvre into the

Right: Cdr. Kleeman (right) and Lt. Venlet – pilot and RIO of "Fast Eagle 102" – re-enact their combat with one of the Libyan SU–22s for the benefit of the media.

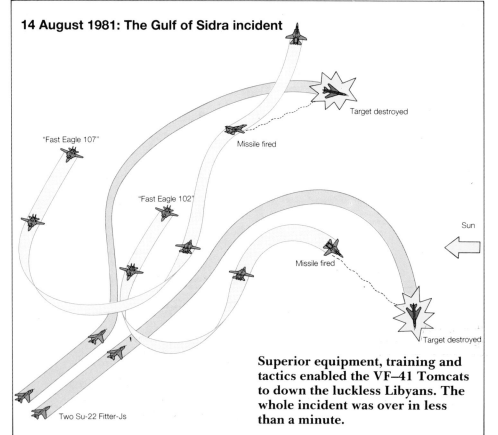

14 August 1981: The Gulf of Sidra incident

"Fast Eagle 107"

"Fast Eagle 102"

Missile fired

Target destroyed

Missile fired

Target destroyed

Sun

Two Su–22 Fitter-Js

Superior equipment, training and tactics enabled the VF–41 Tomcats to down the luckless Libyans. The whole incident was over in less than a minute.

Libyans' six o'clock position, events took on a more serious note. At that moment, both American pilots saw the leading Sukhoi launch a missile – almost certainly a heat-seeking AA–2 Atoll aimed at Kleeman – but this failed to track, passing harmlessly beneath "Fast Eagle 102".

IN PURSUIT

Since US rules of engagement permitted fire to be returned, the Tomcat pilots went on to the offensive, and they were now extremely well positioned, having moved into the rear quadrant of both Fitters. In the lead aircraft, Kleeman's first instinct was to pursue the fighter that had fired and which was still heading out to sea. Within moments, however, he realized that Musczynski was nicely set up to engage that aircraft, so he reversed direction and set off after the enemy wingman who had performed a 180deg turn and made a break for the mainland.

Hot in pursuit, Kleeman readied an AIM–9L Sidewinder AAM, but had sufficient presence of mind to wait a few seconds while the Fitter moved clear of the sun before letting fly at less than a mile's (1.6km) range. The missile homed perfectly, striking the tail unit of the Fitter, which popped its drag 'chute and rolled out of control. Five seconds after being hit, the pilot ejected from his doomed aircraft.

Elsewhere, Musczynski completed a near 180deg turn which put the lead Sukhoi out in front, at more or less the ideal 12 o'clock position. Converting his height advantage to speed by diving, he pounced, closing to half-a-mile (0.8km) before launching a single AIM–9L. This, too, guided perfectly, disappearing into the Sukhoi's exhaust nozzle. The ensuing detonation was evidently quite spectacular, causing the tail section to break away while the rest of the aircraft went into an uncontrollable spin. Although the pilot was seen to eject, no parachute was observed.

From start to finish, the encounter lasted no more than a minute but the ramifications were more enduring. Not surprisingly, Colonel Gadaffi soon made his displeasure evident, but it is doubtful if the Americans were too impressed with his rhetoric although they certainly took note of terrorist activities.

For the Tomcat crews, their exploits earned them brief notoriety on the world stage. For the Tomcat itself, the encounter provided an opportunity to test its mettle in combat, and it certainly wasn't found wanting; good news for the Navy and Grumman which had been targets for a great deal of criticism over the years.

Seven years later, in the closing days of the Reagan administration, US–Libyan relations remained dismal, but military confrontation had been avoided since the 1986 bombing of Tripoli and Benghazi. Nevertheless, there was much speculation in the final weeks of 1988 about the possibility of US air power being used to destroy

a suspected chemical weapons plant at Rabta. As it turned out, those who predicted another "exchange of views" were correct, although nobody seems to have anticipated its form.

Once again, the Tomcat was intimately involved and once again it was to demonstrate its superiority over Libyan equipment. This time, the victims were a pair of MiG–23 Floggers, but although the end result was the same, the circumstances were significantly different. For a start, the American pilots did not wait to be fired upon before they took action, but it should be noted that they were under no obligation to do so, for the rules of engagement had been changed in the intervening period. Now, evidence of aggressive intent was all that was

needed, and that was apparently the case on 4 January 1989.

Whatever the intentions of the Libyan pilots, they paid heavily for their indiscretion, two Tomcat crews from VF–32 aboard the USS *John F. Kennedy* being responsible for the destruction of both aircraft. On this occasion, one fell victim to an AIM–7 Sparrow radar-guided AAM, while the other was destroyed by an AIM–9 Sidewinder AAM. Both pilots were seen to eject before the Tomcats departed the scene.

Leaving aside the question of unfavourable publicity, about the only unsatisfactory aspect was the poor performance of the Sparrow. During the final stages of the eight-minute encounter over the Mediterranean,

FLEET DISTRIBUTION

UNITED STATES NAVY

Atlantic Fleet		Pacific Fleet	
Shore Base: NAS Oceana, Virginia		Shore Base: NAS Miramar, California	
VF–11	"Red Rippers"	VF–1	"Wolfpack"
VF–14	"Top Hatters"	VF–2	"Bounty Hunters"
VF–31	"Tom Catters"	VF–21	"Freelancers"
VF–32	"Swordsmen"	VF–24	"Fighting Renegades"
VF–33	"Starfighters"	VF–51	"Screaming Eagles"
VF–41	"Black Aces"	VF–111	"Sundowners"
VF–74	"Bedevilers"	VF–114	"Aardvarks"
VF–84	"Jolly Rogers"	*VF–124	"Gunfighters"
*VF–101	"Grim Reapers"	VF–154	"Black Knights"
VF–102	"Diamondbacks"	VF–211	"Fighting Checkmates"
VF–103	"Sluggers"	VF–213	"Black Lions"
VF–142	"Ghost Riders"		
VF–143	"Pukin' Dogs"		
* = Atlantic Fleet Replacement Squadron		* = Pacific Fleet Replacement Squadron	

NAVAL AIR RESERVE		TEST AND EVALUATION UNITS
Atlantic Fleet		Naval Air Test Center
Shore Base: NAS Dallas, Texas		NAS Patuxent River, Maryland
VF–201	"Hunters"	Naval Air Engineering Center
VF–202	"Fighting Superheats"	NAEC Lakehurst, New Jersey
		Pacific Missile Test Center
Pacific Fleet		NAS Point Mugu, California
Shore Base: NAS Miramar, California		VX–4 "Evaluators"
VF–301	"Devil's Disciples"	NAS Point Mugu, California
VF–302	"Stallions"	

Tomcat in Service

three Sparrows were fired: two missed for reasons which have not been made public, but the cryptic comment "Aw Jesus" made a few seconds after the first was launched could well have been the exasperated remark of a pilot who had just observed a major malfunction. Evidence to support that conclusion is provided by the fact that a second Sparrow was launched before the first should have reached its target, although the latter missile could well have been aimed at the second Flogger. Either way, both weapons missed, an occurrence which is hardly likely to inspire increased confidence in the Sparrow AAM.

Other combat opportunities also came the way of the Tomcat during the 1980s, most notably in connection with events in the Lebanon. This activity, peaked in the latter half of 1983,

with Tomcats from the USS *Eisenhower* (VF–142/-143), USS *John F. Kennedy* (VF–11/-31) and USS *Independence* (VF–14/-32) performing combat air patrols to prevent Syrian Air Force MiGs from interfering with carrier-borne strike elements. There were no incidents of direct confrontation, although F–14s did come under fire from ground forces. Another mission was reconnaissance, with TARPS-configured F–14As repeatedly surveying enemy positions in the vicinity of Beirut. Again, the Syrian Air Force avoided combat but artillery and missile fire was often encountered, happily without dire consequences for the F–14s and their crews.

For VF–14 and VF–32, operations in the Lebanon followed hard on the heels of another military adventure, this time in Uncle Sam's "back-yard".

Above: Armed with AIM–9L Sidewinder and AIM–7F Sparrow AAMs, a VF–74 "Bedevilers" Tomcat is readied prior to the start of another BarCAP sortie.

On that occasion, the objective was the Caribbean island of Grenada, US concern over the political situation being compounded by the presence of Cuban military personnel, advisers and manual workers. With the situation evidently worsening almost daily, and with other Caribbean nations requesting assistance, the US moved decisively, launching Operation "Urgent Fury" on 24 October 1983.

Involving elements from all of the US armed forces, "Urgent Fury" achieved its objectives within days, although it was not until 2 November that hostilities finally terminated. By then, the USS *Independence* was on the verge of leaving, its contribution being mainly confined to the provision of close air support (CAS) for ground forces. A–6E Intruders and A–7E Corsair IIs were responsible for the CAS mission, but they were not the only Navy aircraft involved, F–14As from VF–14 and VF–32 flying CAP cover. The latter squadron's reconnaissance-configured Tomcats also undertook photo-mapping and post-strike bomb damage assessment missions.

IRANIAN ACTION

If US Navy Tomcats were only sporadically called upon to face combat, those of Iran were in action much more frequently if the sketchy reports of the Gulf War are to be believed. Border clashes between Iran and Iraq began in May 1979, with a gradual worsening of relations culminating in full-blown war in September 1980, when Iraqi forces invaded Iran. One might have expected the better-equipped Iraqis to have gained the ascendancy, but they were perhaps not prepared for the fanaticism shown by Iranian troops. As a result, most of the lost territory was quickly regained and a state of stalemate soon existed, relieved by periodic offensives and counter-offensives intended to bring about "final victory". That "final victory" was to prove elusive, and the eventual ceasefire came after nearly a decade of war which brought misery to millions of people.

Tomcat involvement in the Iran–Iraq war was minimal during the first few years, when most Islamic Republic of Iran Air Force (IRIAF) F–14s were evidently grounded. Lack of spares and insufficient technical expertise were given as the reasons by sources in the Pentagon which believed that the few airworthy machines were being employed primarily as airborne early warning (AEW) platforms. By using the AWG–9 radar to monitor airspace in the vicinity of the border, they would, hopefully, detect low-flying Iraqi warplanes in time for friendly fighters to be scrambled.

Subsequently, it became clear that this estimate of IRIAF Tomcat capability erred on the conservative side, with perhaps the most telling evidence to the contrary coming in early 1985 when 25 Tomcats were reported to have been among 79 aircraft which took part in a mass flypast over Tehran. Of course, just how many of those Tomcats were fully operational is a matter for conjecture, for there is a world of difference between having a flyable aircraft and one that is fully operationally capable.

Below: Though wearing the insignia of the United States, this is one of 79 F–14As exported to Iran.

Further indications that Iran's Tomcat fleet was rather more numerous than at first thought came from the opposition, which was doing its level best to reduce the size of that fleet still further. In that respect, Iraq seems to have achieved some success, pilots claiming to have downed F–14s in aerial combat engagements.

The first such report pre-dates March 1982, when a captured IRIAF pilot evidently revealed in interrogation that an Iraqi MiG–21 had shot down an F–14, much to the surprise of the Iranians. Further combat reports indicate that Iraq may well have accounted for more of Iran's Tomcats in 1983–84, but a clear reading of the exact state of play is unlikely to be forthcoming, since Iran has consistently maintained a policy of silence with regard to losses sustained in the long-running air war.

INDEX